WE CAN STOP THE RAIN!

M. D. Hamm

ISBN 979-8-89243-151-4 (paperback)
ISBN 979-8-89243-152-1 (digital)

Christian Faith Publishing
832 Park Avenue
Meadville, PA 16335
www.christianfaithpublishing.com

Printed in the United States of America

INTRODUCTION

The Bible tells us (Amos 5:18–20) not to desire the day of the Lord. This book explains why and tells you what needs to be done. These Amos scriptures end with a question mark because we can change a day of sadness into a day of gladness and great celebration.

We can stop the rain!

CHAPTER 1

Hello, My Friend

I lived my life filled with addiction and sin. I feel like I am the last person on earth whom God should choose to help save humanity. I often wonder why God would think anyone would believe me, and yet here we are!

I have quite an amazing story to tell you. I have witnessed God's glorious light, and I am now a humble servant of our Lord and Savior Jesus Christ. My name is Michael, and this is my testimony.

I have experienced what I like to call the Noah Event. During two visits, an angel sent by God gave me information and told me to write this book for you. For years, a puzzle nagged at me. Why would someone bury their home before they left? On September 17, 2019, the answer popped into my head so fast, it almost knocked me over. This was the beginning of the angel's first visit.

For the next four days and four nights, I received information about Noah and the great flood. The angel showed me that the story of Noah's Ark is a true story. Noah was a righteous man in the eyes of God, and he was also a great scientist. Noah used DNA technology to fit the animals onto the ark. An ancient version of Noah's story tells us that the "seed" of every animal was carried onto the Ark. The seed is referring to DNA technology. The angel also showed me that Noah's story is part 1 of a two-part warning.

Noah built for us and buried a gigantic sign so we would know that the global flood described in the Bible is a reoccurring event. The flood reoccurs because planet earth is a broken greenhouse. The daily news shows us that deadly and devastating storms have been growing in size, strength, and intensity. These weather patterns are occurring more and more frequently all over the planet and will continue to get worse.

On September 27, 2019, the angel showed up again. The second visit lasted four hours, and I knew that my life would never be the same. The next day, thoughts of doubt entered my mind. I began to wonder if the two events were real until I bought a Bible and realized there was a connection my mind could not have known. My mother was born on the seventeenth day, the angel's first visit began on the seventeenth day, and on the twenty-seventh day of the month, the angel showed me God and gave me the answers we need to fix our planet. The Bible tells us that the rain began on the seventeenth day, the Ark came to rest on the seventeenth day, and on the twenty-seventh day of the month, God told Noah to open the Ark and to go forth onto the earth. When I saw the dates in the Bible, I knew the events I had experienced were very, very real. Also, the information I had received made so much sense that I knew it could not be wrong.

I was also reminded that I had always had a strong feeling of intuition my entire life that I was born for the purpose of writing a book. I now had the topic of the book, and I knew the plan for me to write this book was in place before my mother was even born!

Sixty-six million years ago, God sent the asteroid named Chicxulub hurling through outer space and slammed it into Mexico's Yucatán Peninsula. God did this because the extinction of the dinosaur was necessary to pave the way for mankind's existence. By doing so, God also destroyed the rainforest, causing the reoccurring global flood to begin, thus creating the ultimate test for mankind. The prevention of our own extinction!

I can explain the how, the why, and what we need to do to prevent the future flood, but let me start by showing you the sign Noah built for you and me. I am in awe of Noah. He could not save the people of his time, so he spent the rest of his life trying to save us!

Have you ever heard of a place called Göbekli Tepe? The odd thing about Tepe is the builders buried their home before they left!

Noah's Warning, the Sign

In the 1990s, a farmer in Turkey found a large stone protruding from the ground. Little did the farmer know, it would be the greatest archeological discovery in our modern history. The fact that Mount Ararat is nearby and the timing of the farmer's discovery are not coincidences. Mount Ararat is where the Bible tells us Noah's Ark landed and the future flood is rapidly approaching.

Archeologists began to dig and have named the site Göbekli Tepe; please google "Göbekli Tepe" at any time. I would like for you to see the sign that Noah built for us with your own eyes!

Tepe has been dated to about 10,000 BC. That means Tepe is a postflood pre–Stone Age site. Tepe consists of large stone pillars with carvings on them. The pillars are arranged in circle after circle and so on and so on; there are many circles.

Each circle contains twelve carved stones. Most of the carvings consist of species of animals from all over the world, not just that area. There are also carvings of humans wearing sophisticated clothing.

Some people theorize that Tepe proves experts wrong about the Stone Age. That theory is wrong. Tepe proves that Arks cannot prevent the Stone Age.

Tepe is in pristine condition because the builders of Tepe intentionally buried it before they left. Why would someone bury their home before they leave? There is only one correct answer. They are trying to leave people in the distant future a message. Burying the carved stones is the only way to keep Mother Nature and Father Time from erasing the carvings.

The carvings and the time that Tepe was built along with the children's story and Bible story tell us that Göbekli Tepe was built by Noah. The stories tell us Noah survived a global flood.

The circles tell us what happened before will happen again. The global flood is a reoccurring event.

That is not the only thing the circle tells us. The circle also tells us that the circle can be broken. There is no point in the warning unless the future flood can be prevented.

Göbekli Tepe is a warning sign built for us and buried by Noah and his descendants. The carvings are a recorded inventory of the animals and insects Noah carried on the Ark. Before I explain the stories and offer you proof, I should show you that the future flood is very, very real!

The Key

How our planet works is very complicated. However, planet earth is a gigantic greenhouse, and basic greenhouse principles still apply. Here is the basic greenhouse principle in its simplest form:

Raise temperature (global warming) + add water (oceans rising)
= water everywhere, not a dry spot in our greenhouse!

This process keeps occurring over and over because our planet is out of balance. The key to understanding is answering the question, why are the oceans and deserts growing at the same time?

Here is the answer: Scientists tell us that when the dinosaurs lived the rainforests were three times larger, and earth's atmosphere was much more tropical. The asteroid that killed the dinosaurs also killed the rainforests. This immediately caused the very first ice age to occur. What followed next, after some time, was the first global flood.

When the flood occurs, it's because it starts to rain and does not stop. All that rain comes from the moisture in the air. Immediately following the flood, a new ice age is ushered in, and a very large amount of water is frozen. However, when the ice melts, the water goes into our oceans and not back into the atmosphere, where the moisture comes from.

Every single time the flood occurs, the earth's climate becomes less tropical and more of a drier climate. This explains why the oceans and deserts are both growing and also why the landmass is shrinking.

Puzzle Pieces of Evidence

Here are pieces of evidence that experts in various fields consider modern-day puzzles. All the puzzle pieces fit together one way and one way only: a reoccurring flood!

The evidence:

1. Lack of evidence from humanity's past
2. Sunken cities found all over the world
3. Fossils of ocean creatures found in the highest elevations of the world
4. Oceans and deserts growing at the same time
5. A two-part warning left for us by Noah
6. Ancient texts in India
7. Ancient sites built by humans that predate the Stone Age
8. The reoccurring ice age

Now let me explain: The global rain blocks out the sun and significantly cools the global temperature. Every time the flood occurs, a new ice age is what follows. When we prevent the flood, the ice age will also be prevented!

Ancient sites that predate the Stone Age do not prove experts wrong about the Stone Age. Those ancient sites prove that the Stone

Age cannot be prevented with arks. They also prove that humanity has repeated the Stone Age!

Ancient texts in India describe cities and technology from thirty thousand years ago. Those texts were considered myths until a tsunami exposed cities matching exact descriptions on the ocean floor. Those texts are now considered historical documents. The evidence proves they are not myths!

Noah's story lets us know to look for evidence of the past floods. Noah's sign points to and warns us of the flood in our near future. The oceans and deserts both growing are absolute proof that our greenhouse planet is broken.

The reason we find fossils of ocean-dwelling creatures at our highest elevations is very simple. Every time the floodwaters recede, those creatures become trapped on land and die. Those receding waters also explain the lack of evidence from humanity's past. The oceans rising explains the sunken cities.

Separately these puzzles remain unexplainable. When you put them all together, the reoccurring flood answers them. There are many more puzzle pieces that are solved by the reoccurring flood. Let me explain the unicorn in Noah's warning. For centuries, scholars have been trying to solve the unicorn puzzle.

The Unicorn

The unicorn is only mentioned in the children's story, not the Bible.

The reason for this is very simple: the Bible is all truth.

The unicorn is a fictional (made-up) character with a point. Hence, the one horn is Noah telling us to pay attention to the unicorn because there is a point to the story.

Let me refresh your memory of how the story goes: The unicorn was a very timid creature. When Noah put all of the animals onto the Ark, he realized that the unicorn was not among them. Noah knew the unicorn's timid nature was causing it to hide in the woods. Noah could not see the unicorn, but he knew the unicorn could hear him, and he knew the unicorn was watching him.

Noah tried and tried to coax the unicorn out of the woods and onto the Ark, but the unicorn would not come. Sadly, Noah had no choice but to leave the unicorn behind. The timid nature of the unicorn is what caused the unicorn's extinction.

Now let me explain what Noah is telling us. Noah could not see the unicorn, but he knew the unicorn was there. The unicorn symbolizes the pressure that is building in our atmosphere right now!

We cannot see pressure, but we all know that pressure exists. The unicorn's point is extinction. Noah is telling us that if we do not release the pressure that is building in our atmosphere, then all land-dwelling species on planet earth will become extinct.

Purpose of the Rainforests

How do we make a greenhouse rain? We raise the temperature, add a bucket of water, and shut the door. When we shut the door, pressure immediately starts to build and keeps building until the water in the bucket evaporates and reforms on the ceiling and in the air as droplets of water.

The end result is rain everywhere in the greenhouse.

Rain everywhere on our planet (all at once) is not a good thing. This is where the rainforest is needed. The daily rain provided by the rainforests releases the pressure in our atmosphere.

The rainforests must be large enough to maintain a balance and keep the basic greenhouse principle from occurring.

We can fix our planet by building rainforests. When we do this, the oceans and deserts will shrink, and the landmass will grow. We can prevent the future flood, but we must start now.

Our generation is the last. The next generation is too late!

CHAPTER 7

The Vision

Near the end of the angel's visit, I received a vision. I was standing in the back of a huge auditorium. In the room were all of our world leaders.

They all had their backs to me, except for one. The leader of China was facing me.

The topic of discussion was the future flood. They knew that what I am telling you is the truth. Some of the leaders were yelling, and some of them were silent.

The leaders yelling were arguing about how to pay to fix our planet. The silent leaders were gripped by fear because they believe God will hold them accountable. I realized that their failure to agree had led to a decision.

Our world leaders have decided to build arks in outer space.

Suddenly, the space race is back on with a vengeance, and now you know why! Think about it, every major government, including billionaires, is involved in the current space race.

I was immediately filled with anger and rage. Suddenly I was back in my room. I was completely awestruck by what happened next.

The angel pulled back a curtain. I was looking at the most beautiful, most awesome, most magnificent, and most glorious light in the universe. I was looking at God's light, and he spoke these words to me: "It is wrong for us to judge others. When we do, we are stepping over a line that we should not cross!"

The curtain immediately closed, and then I learned the fate of the world leaders if they do not start fixing our planet. Basically, the greatest moment of my life was followed by the worst feeling of my life.

My anger and rage were immediately washed away by the most horrible and overwhelming feeling of sorrow. I was shaking, crying, and had knots in my stomach, for the sake of the elect, until I fell asleep.

When I awoke, that feeling was still there and stuck with me for months. Our leaders' fate is so terrible that I had to block it out of my mind. They will be punished for every life that is lost to the flood. Those deaths will be distributed evenly. All of the leaders will receive the same punishment. If any person murders a world leader, that person will receive all of their punishment combined.

They still have a chance to change their fate. God is their judge, not us!

CHAPTER 8

Arks Won't Work

Noah's warning tells us that humanity has repeated the Stone Age at least three times. We know this because Noah was looking at the same puzzles we see today.

The main reason arks cannot prevent the Stone Age is the average life expectancy. In the 1800s, the average life span was twenty to thirty years old. The most common cause of death was falling off your horse and hitting your head.

This saying says it all: "With age comes wisdom and knowledge!" Every time a person dies, knowledge will be lost. We could stockpile the moon, but eventually those supplies would dwindle.

The flood's raging currents will erase the world we live in today.

Transportation will be useless because there will be no place to go. There will be nothing left to salvage. The supplies will be irreplaceable.

Why did Noah build the Ark out of wood? Noah knew that he would need the wood for heat because of the ice age that followed the flood.

Noah lived for over nine centuries, and Noah knew that he could not prevent the average life span from returning us to the Stone Age.

Noah is telling us that if we build arks, we will become extinct. It's all in the warning!

CHAPTER 9

The Answers

The next morning, the angel was gone. I realized right away that the answers to fixing our broken greenhouse had been seared into my memory. This is what we need to do: We must start planting trees one acre at a time on four or five deserts simultaneously. Every time we finish an acre, we start a new acre right next to the one we just finished. We need to do this as fast as we can for two hundred years.

After two hundred years, we can stop because Mother Nature will take over and do the rest. We need to build rainforests.

The rainforests need to be three times larger than our current rainforests were before we started cutting them down. Everyone in the world could plant a tree in his or her backyard, and it would not work. We must build rainforests to release the pressure and maintain a balance in our gigantic greenhouse.

We must start now because our generation is the last generation that can prevent the future flood. The next generation is too late!

Noah's Warning, the Proof

Why does the Bible tell us the dimensions of Noah's Ark? Experts consider this another puzzle. This puzzle has two answers.

1. Noah's age tells us that they had better technology than we do today. The size of the Ark tells us that Noah had to have had DNA technology for the animals to fit. An ancient version of Noah's story tells us that the "seed" of every animal was carried onto the Ark.

2. Noah left us the specifications we need so we could prove the reoccurring flood in a model-scale greenhouse. Here is an outline to build your model with step-by-step instructions. Every time we make a greenhouse rain, we prove the flood. This model proves the oceans growing and landmass disappearing.

The size of your model greenhouse is 300×50×30. Your model has three floors: the sky, the land, and the sea. Your model must be airtight, and you must be able to measure the PSI (unicorn) in your model greenhouse. You must have a window so you can see when the rainbow appears. Finally, you must be able to freeze your model and heat your model to 350 degrees.

Once you have built your model, we can begin! Here are your other numbers 7, 40, 600, 350, 150, 10, and 950. Your model needs 40 percent land and 60 percent sea. That is the 40 and 600. I believe that the extra zero is telling you how much water should be in the model. You will know this because the 60 percent and the 600 measurement of water will correlate to the model's size.

When you turn on your model, let it run for 7 days. You need to get your water into the air. Once you have done this, freeze your model. Once frozen, turn on the heat to 350 degrees. When the rainbow appears, immediately freeze your model again. The rainbow signals the flood is occurring in your model. Keep repeating this process until your landmass is submerged.

You will learn what the 10, 15, 150, and 950 represent as you go. The 150 could be a PSI or a temperature. I have given you a guideline. I am not a scientist or expert in any field. I am just a messenger. I am positive Noah hid the information to prove the flood within the pages of the Bible because it was shown to me.

Anyone who wants to try and prove this can. May God bless you and help you to succeed!

CHAPTER 11

Noah's Warning, the Stories

Noah's story has a children's version and a religious version for specific and very important reasons.

1. The Stone Age presented a major obstacle for Noah. The story having two versions greatly increases the odds of the story's survival.
2. The Bible is all truth. This fact makes different aspects of both versions stand out. Aspects like the unicorn and the dimensions of the ark. Noah's age and DNA technology clearly shows us that in Noah's era, their technology was more advanced than we are today.

When you put the two versions of the story together along with Noah's sign, a more complete story emerges. Let me remind you that the circles at Göbekli Tepe tell us that history repeats itself. This is what happened in Noah's era.

A scientist named Noah realized a global flood was reoccurring and also realized that the future flood could be prevented. Noah did not want to cause panic, so he met with his world leaders in private and told them all that he had discovered. The leaders argued about who should pay to fix the planet, and they could not agree, so they decided to build arks for themselves!

Noah was shocked and stunned by the fact that his leaders would even consider any option other than fixing the planet, so he tried to tell the world the truth, but it was too late. The leaders smeared Noah's good name and made him appear crazy to the rest of the world.

The leaders had forgotten that God was always watching. The leaders were so drunk with power and conceit that they could not see the fact that God was always in control.

God was already upset because angels mated with human women, and the wickedness of man was great all over the earth, and evil thoughts were in man's heart continually. The actions of the leaders were the final straw that broke the camel's back.

God decided to make the flood happen sooner and cleanse the earth of all evil. God told Noah his plan, and when Noah was finished preparing, God sent a meteor shower to melt the ice caps and usher in the flood sooner than expected.

Our scientists have already found evidence that the meteor shower occurred. God did not allow any survivors other than Noah, his wife, and sons and their wives. The Bible is all truth. We are all descendants of Noah.

Noah warned them, and they all died because they would not believe.

I want you to know that your story can have a different ending!

CHAPTER 12

"For God so Loved the World"

I have heard people claim that the earth is six thousand years old. The Bible does not tell us that the earth is six thousand years old. It says, "He remembers his covenant forever, the word that he commanded, for a thousand generations" (Psalm 105:8). This scripture tells us that the amount of time from Adam's creation until the end is one thousand generations. Those who believe already know that the scriptures must and will be fulfilled.

I would like to show you a pattern that cannot be ignored. Sixty-six million years ago, the flood began with the asteroid that caused the extinction of the dinosaurs, God created man on the sixth day, our Stone Age lasted six thousand years, and our modern age goes back six thousand years.

Twelve thousand years have passed since Noah's flood until now. Twelve carved stones make up each circle at Göbekli Tepe. There are twelve tribes of Israel, and there are twelve disciples of our Lord and Savior, Jesus Christ. These are not coincidences, my friend. These are parts of a divine plan designed by our divine creator. Our father in heaven is an all-knowing God. He loves each and every one of us, and he designed his plan with you and me in mind.

"For God so loved the world that he gave his only begotten son" (John 3:16). The Bible tells us, "There is no one righteous, not even one" (Romans 3:10). "Therefore no one will be declared righteous in God's sight" (Romans 3:20 NIV).

Being a good person is not enough to get you into heaven. We have all sinned in the eyes of the lord. The angel told me that writing this book was not a ticket to heaven. Forgiveness and reconciliation is how you get to heaven. You must believe in and accept Jesus Christ as your Lord and Savior with love in your heart.

When I began reading the New Testament, I realized immediately that Jesus Christ truly is the Son of God! I was baptized, and I have accepted Jesus Christ as my Lord and Savior. I believe, I have faith, and I know that my sins are forgiven.

I made a choice! Free will means we all have a choice! Our world leaders can choose to tell the public the truth about the flood, or they can continue to ignore the warning signs. This book is an attempt to help them make the right decision, but the choice is still theirs to make. Fixing our planet begins with telling the public the truth!

Please, do not be alarmed if our leaders refuse because God's plan has you in mind. You too have been given a choice. Noah's world was full of wickedness and evil. Our world is full of wickedness and evil. The time for evil has come to an end!

Those who believe, put their faith in the Lord, and trust in the name of Jesus Christ will live! When the Lord returns, men will trade spears for pruners, the deserts will blossom, and trees will grow in the deserts!

People have told me that I am wrong because God promised to never again destroy the earth with a flood. God's promise is this: "I establish my covenant with you, that never again shall "All" flesh be cut off by the waters of the flood" (Genesis 9:11). When asked about the future, Jesus said, "For as were the days of Noah, so will be the coming of the son of man. For as in those days before the flood they were eating and drinking, marrying and giving in marriage, until the day when Noah entered the Ark, and they were unaware until the flood came and swept them all away, so will be the coming of the son of man. Then two men will be in the field; one will be taken and one left. Two women will be grinding at the mill; one will be taken and one left" (Mathew 24:37–41 ESV). Please read Amos 5:18–20.

God bless every person who believes these words, reads the Bible, and chooses to follow our Lord and Savior, Jesus Christ. The word of our Lord teaches us how to live, to love God, and to love our neighbor!

My name is Michael, and my testimony is true. I believe that our Lord sent me a sign. He wants the leaders to know this can end in two different ways. If they choose to start planting the trees, *we can stop the rain*!

The end!

www.ingramcontent.com/pod-product-compliance
Lightning Source LLC
Chambersburg PA
CBHW020657160726
47991CB00003B/1233